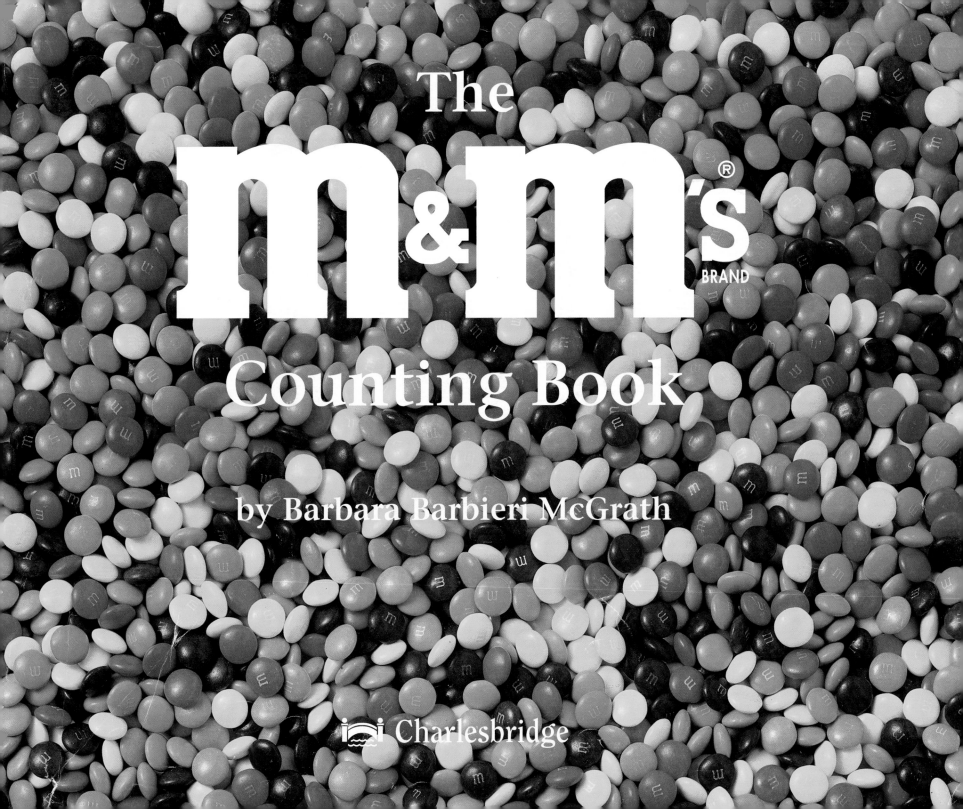

The m&m's® BRAND
Counting Book

by Barbara Barbieri McGrath

Charlesbridge

Easy
McGrath

Consultant to the Editor
Ann Foley, 2nd Grade Teacher
Eisenhower Elementary School, Wauwatosa, Wisconsin

"M&M's," "M," the "M&M's" character and the distinctive packaging for
"M&M's" candies are licensed trademarks of MARS, INCORPORATED.

The exact number of pieces of each color of "M&M's"® Chocolate Candies
may vary from package to package. As a result, there may be insufficient
quantities of each color of "M&M's"® Chocolate Candies in each package to
match the quantity of colors required for play in this book.

Text © 1994
by Barbara Barbieri McGrath
Illustrations © 1994
by Charlesbridge Publishing
All rights reserved, including the right of
reproduction in whole or in part in any form.

Published by
Charlesbridge Publishing
85 Main Street
Watertown, MA 02172-4411
(617) 926-0329

Printed in the United States of America.
(sc) 10 9 8 7 6 5 4 3
(hc) 10 9 8 7 6 5 4 3 2 1

Printed on Recycled Paper.

Library of Congress Cataloging-in-Publication Data
McGrath, Barbara Barbieri.
    The "M&M's"® Brand Counting Book / by Barbara Barbieri
McGrath.
        p.   cm.
    Cover title: The "M&M's"® Brand Counting Book.
    ISBN 0-88106-853-5 (softcover)
    ISBN 0-88106-854-3 (hardcover)
    ISBN 0-88106-855-1 (library reinforced)
    1. Counting — Juvenile literature. 2. Colors — Juvenile
literature. [1. Counting. 2. Color.] I. Title. II. Title: The
"M&M's"® Brand Counting Book.
QA113.B36   1994
[E] — dc20   — dc20
[513.2'11]
                                                    93-35619
                                                    CIP
                                                    AC

The author would like to thank the following people for their assistance and patience,
Will. M., Roger and Dianne G., Albert B. Jr., Joanne B., Jerry P., John B.,
Mary Ann S., Sue S., Drew Y., M and D, and Karen S.

This book is dedicated with love to Will, Emily, and W. Louis —

Barbara Barbieri McGrath

Pour out the candies. Get ready, get set.
This counting book is the tastiest yet!

Call out the colors,
I know you can . . .

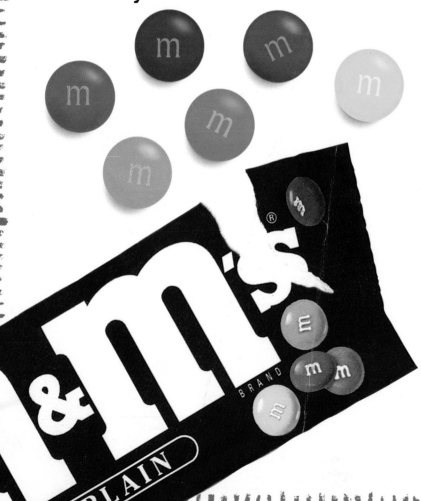

Brown!
Green!
Orange!
Red!
Yellow!
and
Tan!

This certainly is a most colorful mix!
Now sort them as I do and count up to six.

One tan

1
One

Two green

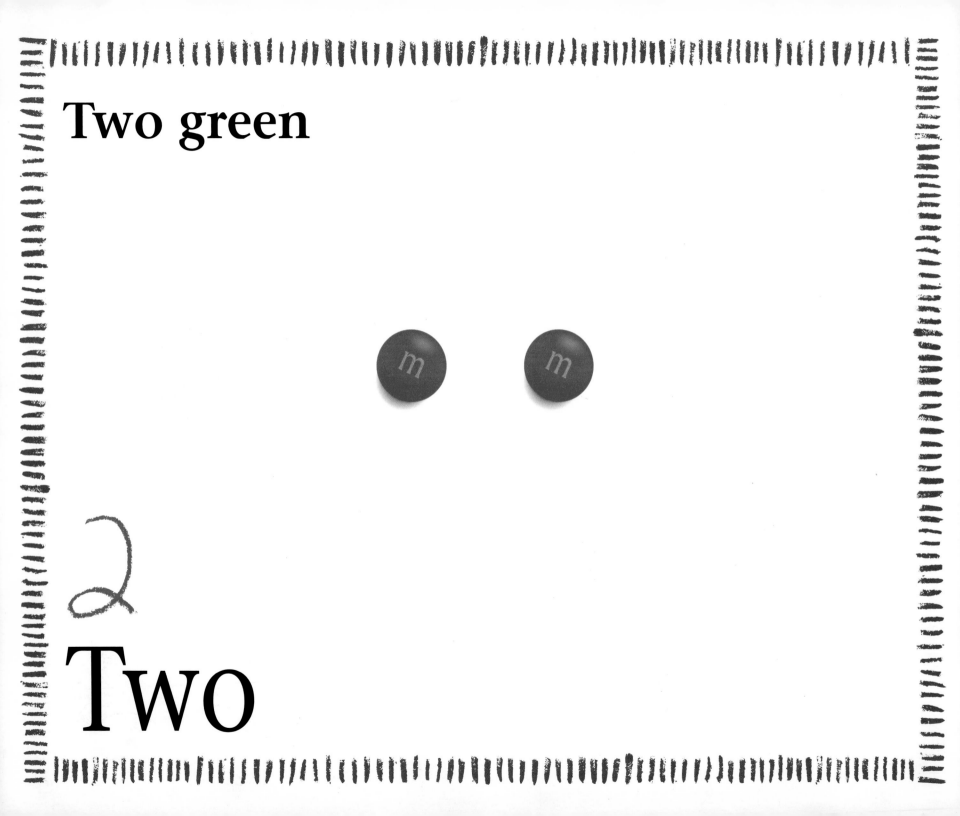

2

Two

Three orange

Let's go.

3

Three

Four yellow

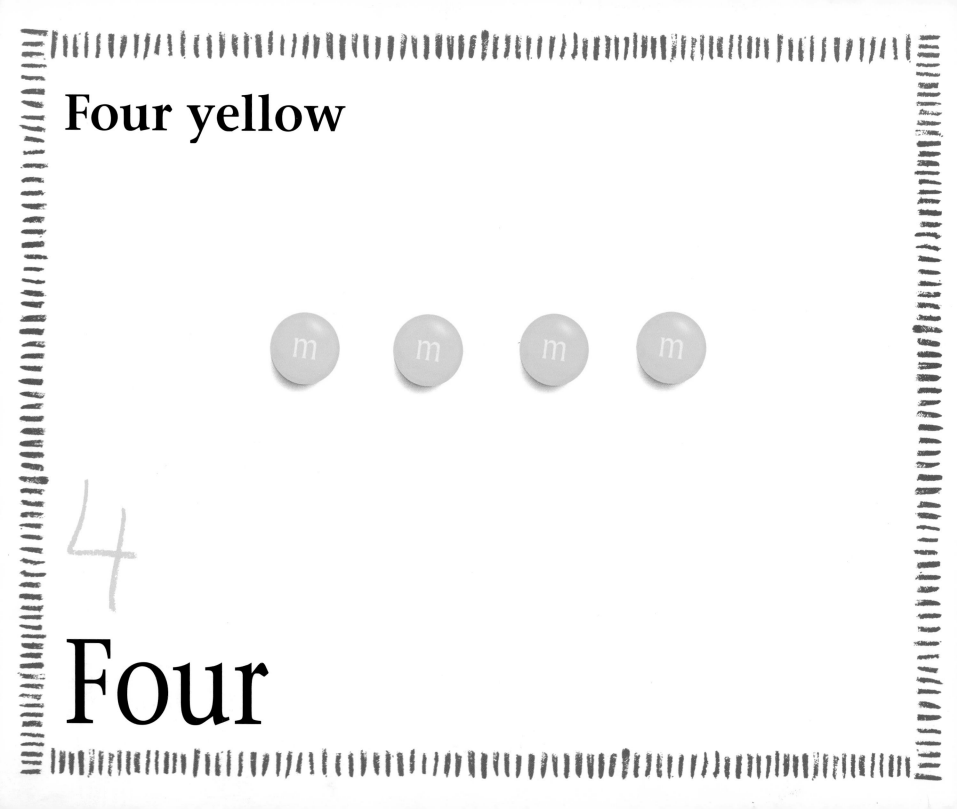

4

Four

Five red

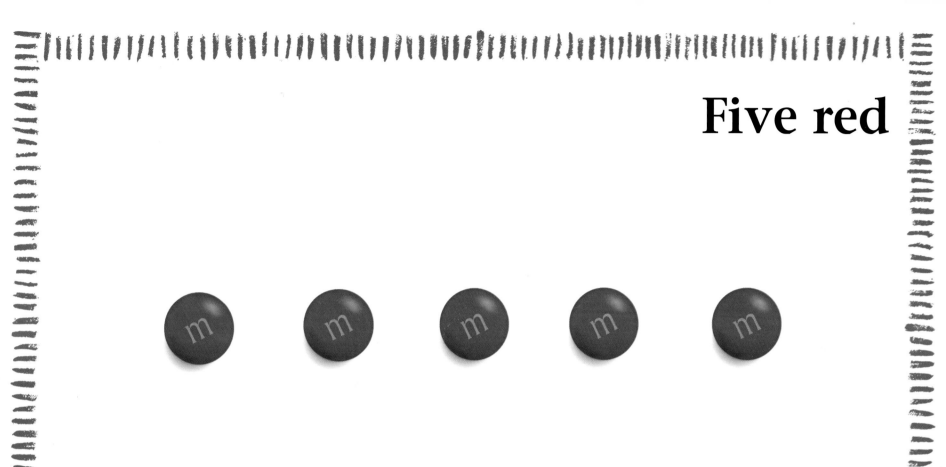

5

Five

Six brown.

Good show!

6

Six

Let's count to twelve now.
That's a dozen, you know.

Keep the six brown. Push the others aside.
Please use these pictures and words as your guide.

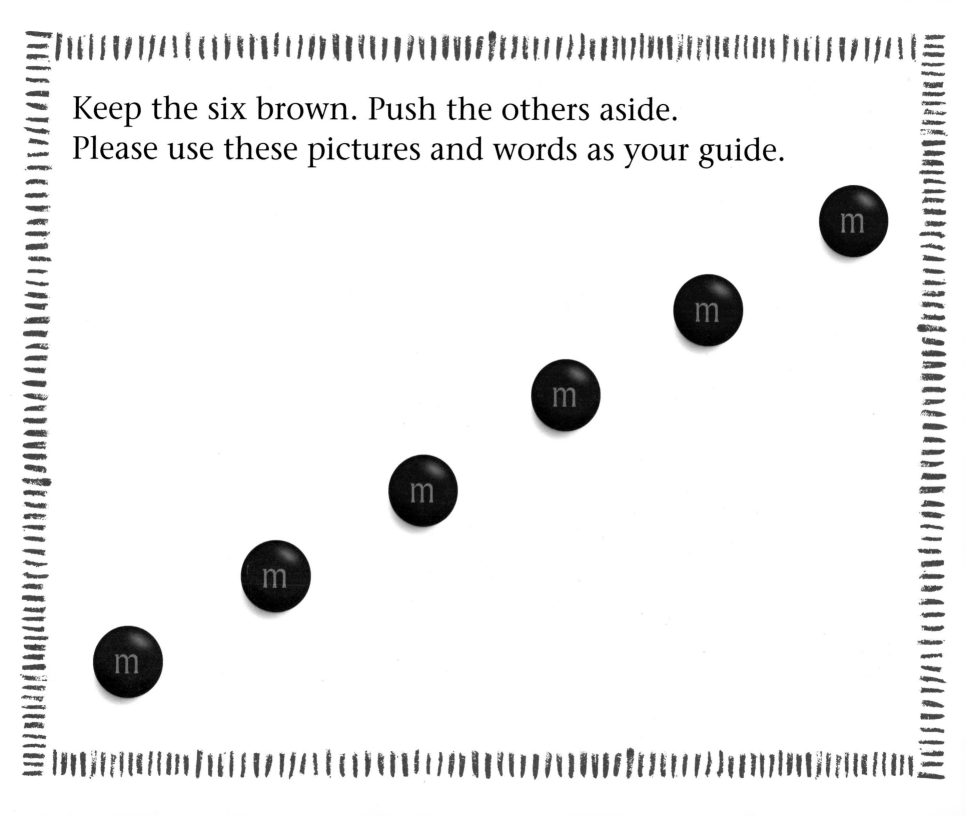

Now add a tan to make seven . . . that's great!

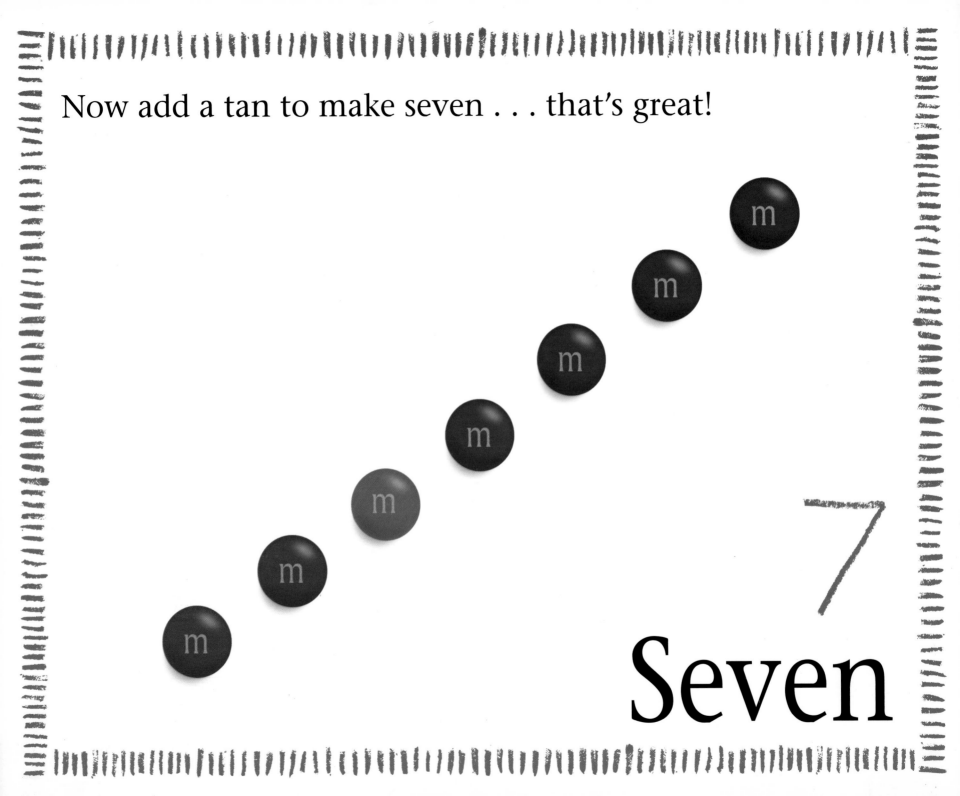

7
Seven

Put a green near the middle. Now you have 8!

8

Eight

Add a red to your group to make nine, and then . . .

9

Nine

Add the orange and now we've already reached ten!

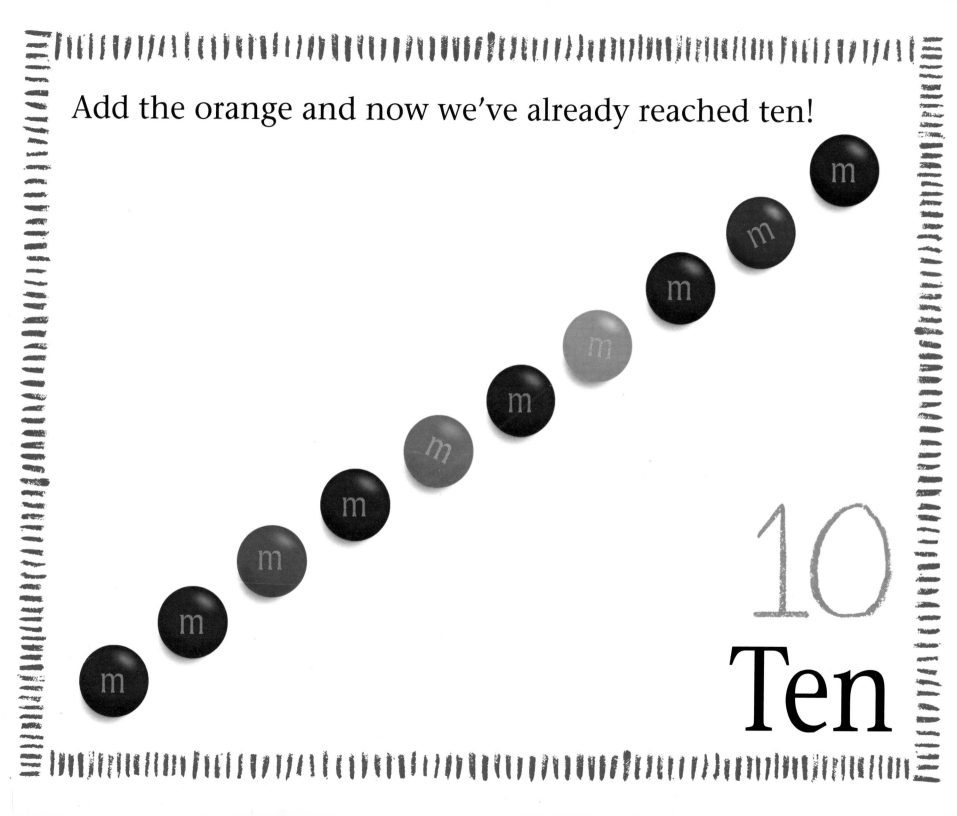

10
Ten

To get to eleven, add a yellow one now.

11

Eleven

Add a brown — that's twelve!
Great work! Take a bow!
You counted to twelve.
I knew that you could!
Want to move on?
I thought that you would!

12
Twelve

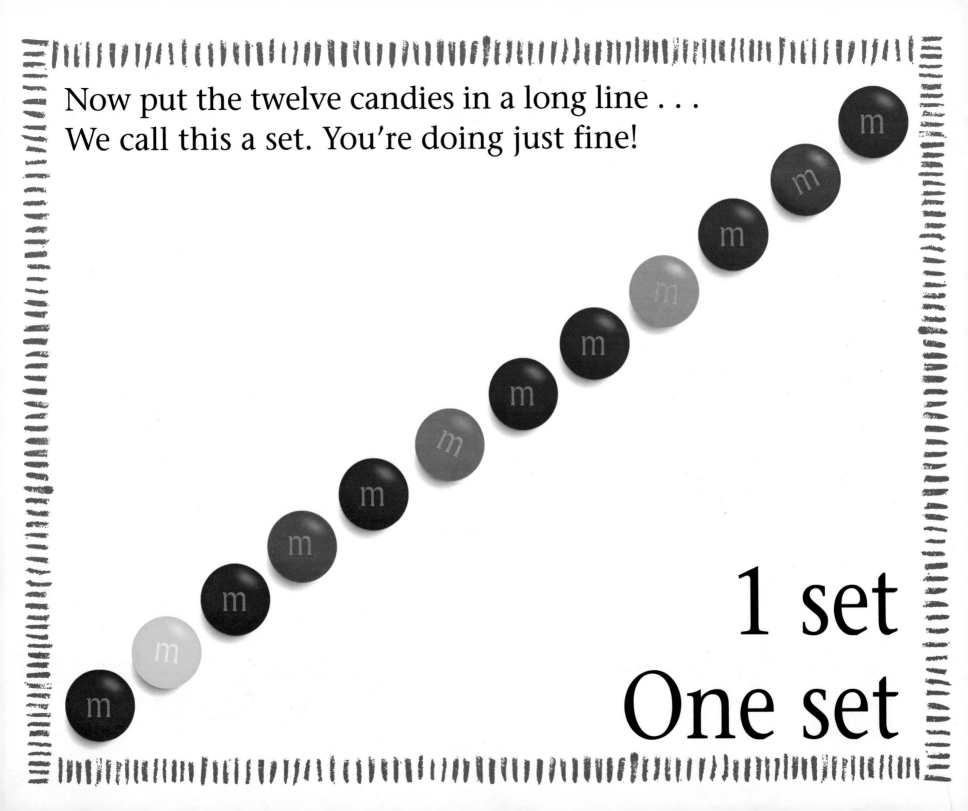

Now put the twelve candies in a long line . . .
We call this a set. You're doing just fine!

1 set
One set

Make six groups of two. That's easy for you.
What does this make? Six sets of two!

$$\begin{array}{r} 2 \\ +2 \\ +2 \\ +2 \\ +2 \\ +2 \\ \hline 12 \end{array}$$

6 sets

Six sets

Change them around to make three sets of four.
Count them. How many? Still twelve and no more!

$$\begin{array}{r} 4 \\ 4 \\ + 4 \\ \hline 12 \end{array}$$

3 sets
Three sets

Now it is time to make four sets of three.
There are still only twelve, as you can see.

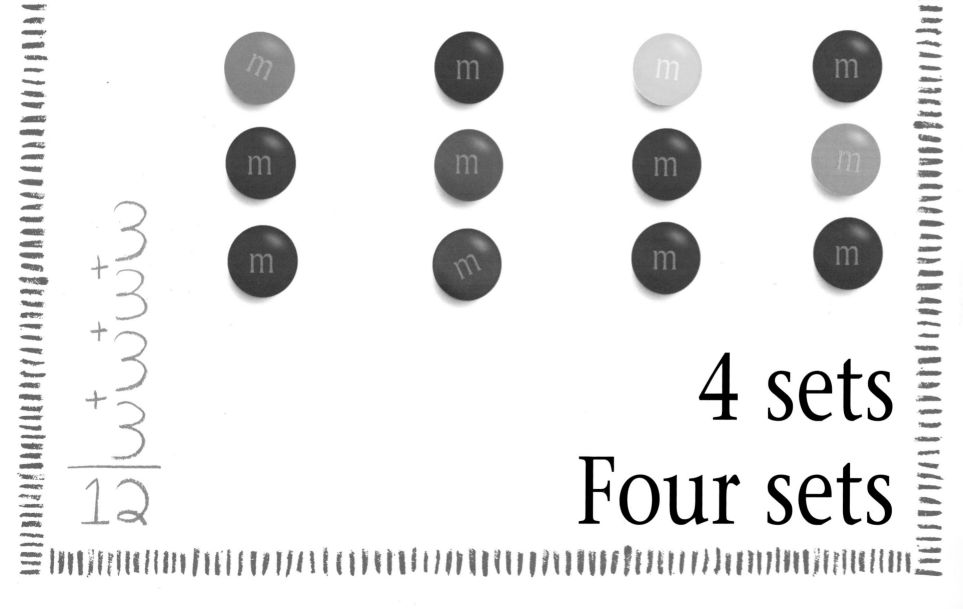

$$\begin{array}{r} 3 \\ 3 \\ 3 \\ + 3 \\ \hline 12 \end{array}$$

4 sets
Four sets

Make two sets of six now. How did you do?
You did that so well — let's start something new.

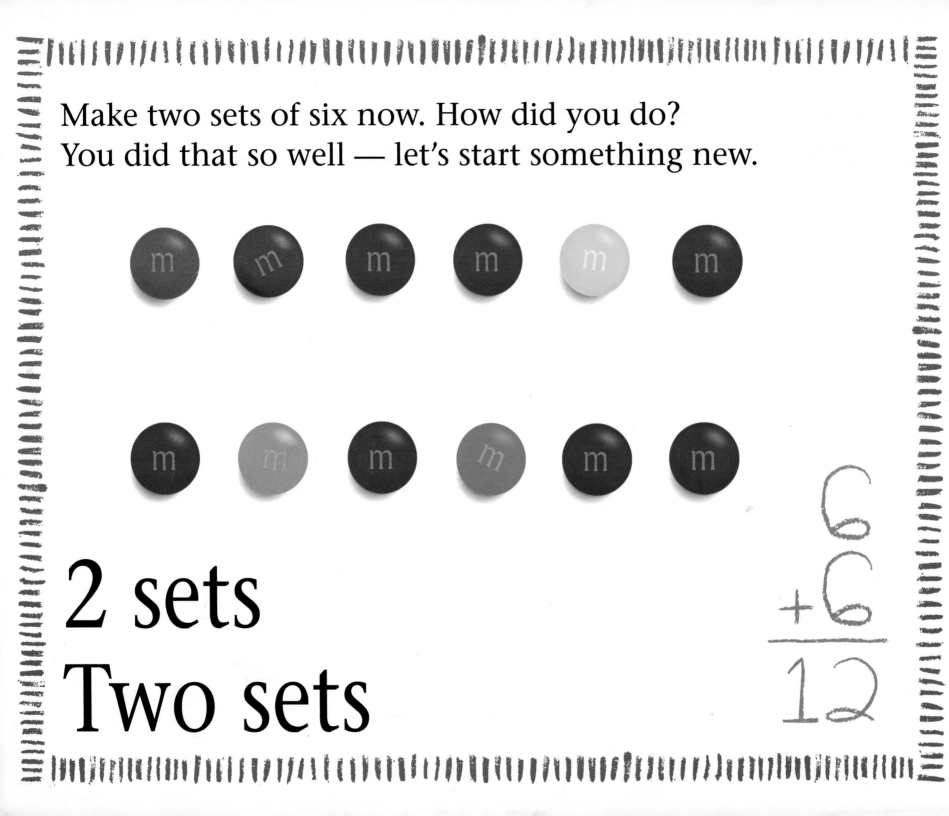

2 sets
Two sets

$$\begin{array}{r} 6 \\ +6 \\ \hline 12 \end{array}$$

Shape the twelve candies, please, into a square.
A square has four sides. Please count them with care.

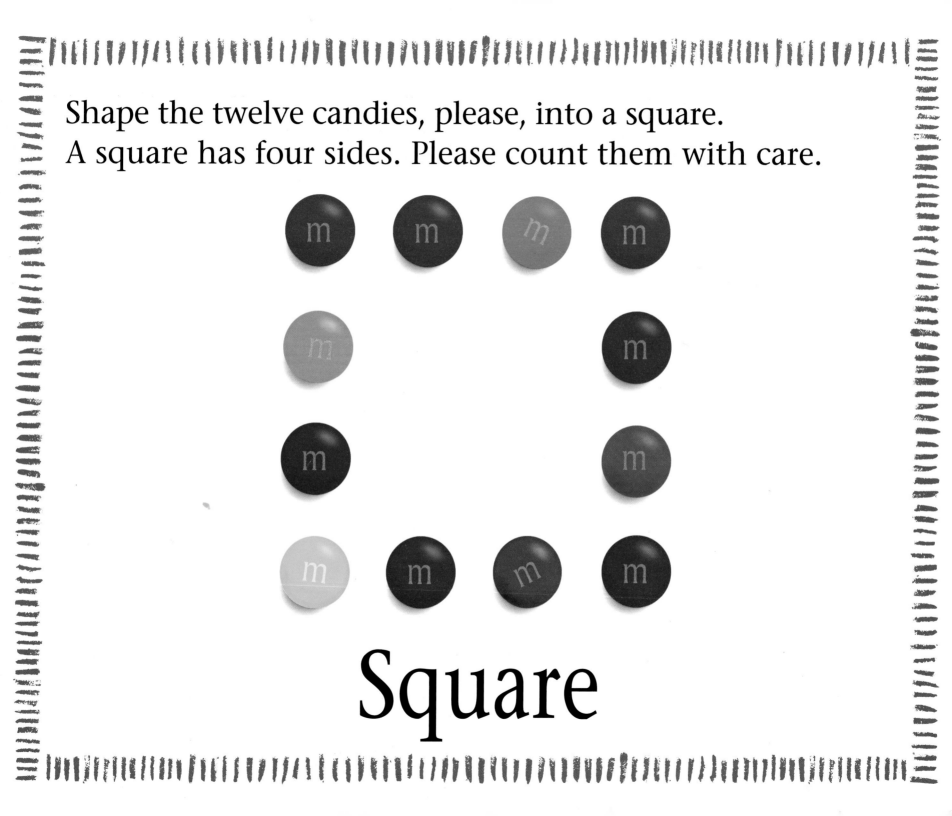

Square

Change the square to a circle, the big round kind.
A circle's beginning is real hard to find.

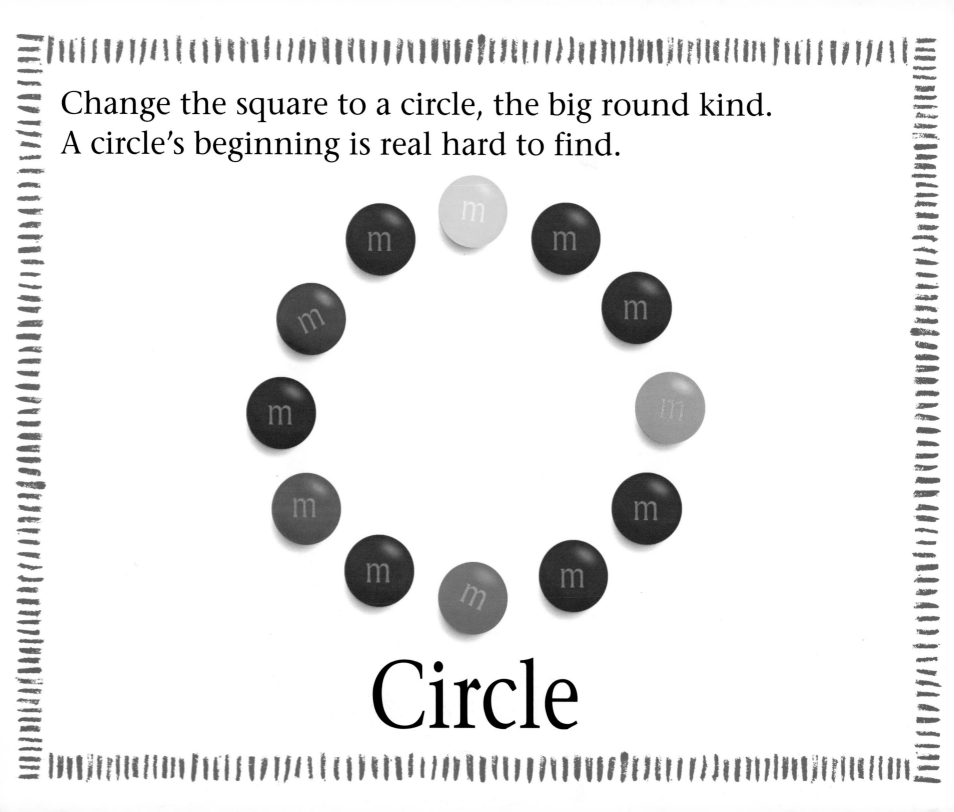

Circle

Let's make a triangle before we stop.
Give it three sides and a point on the top.

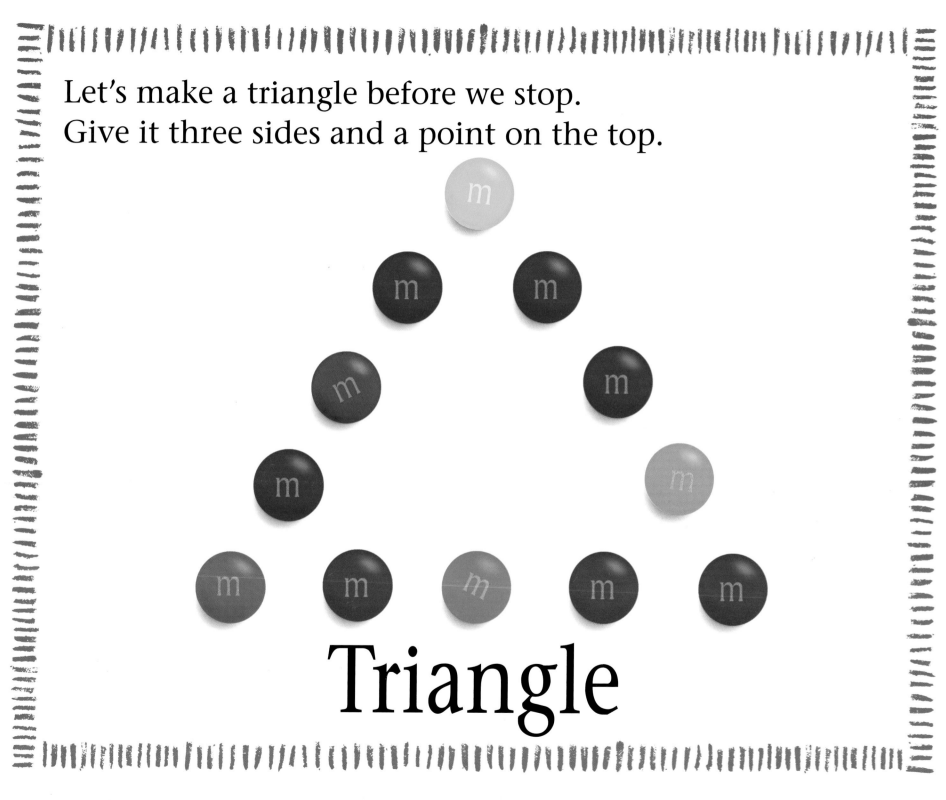

Triangle

Now comes the part that will be the most fun.
We'll start to subtract — so eat the tan one.

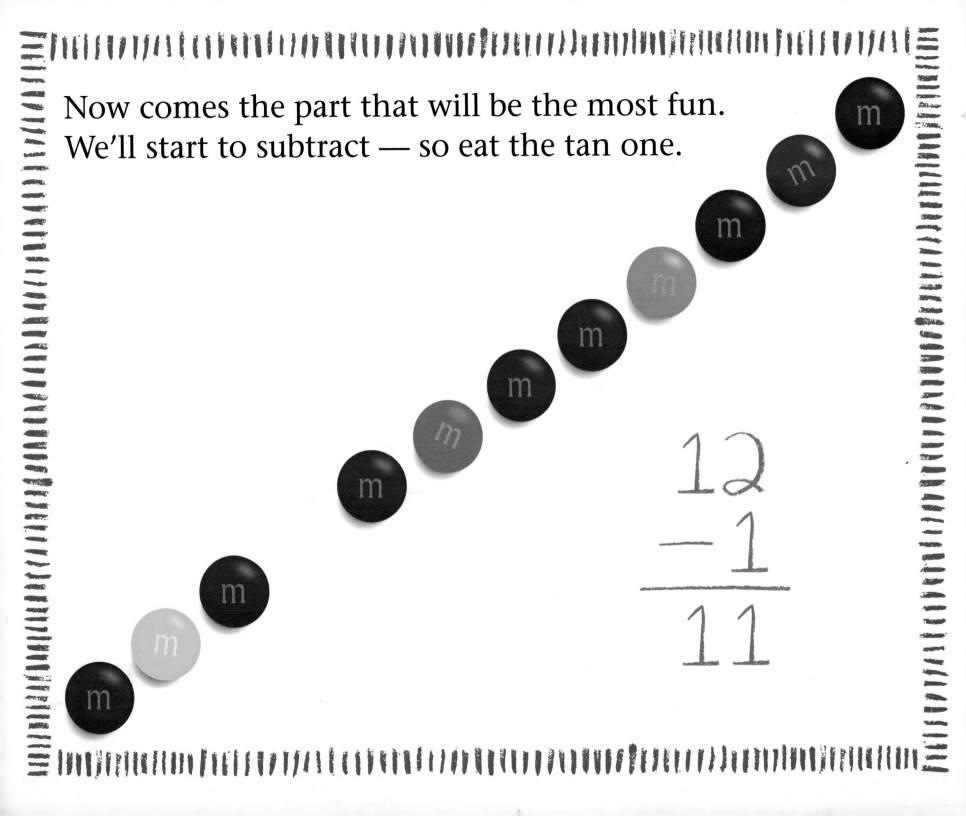

$$\begin{array}{r} 12 \\ -1 \\ \hline 11 \end{array}$$

Count and you'll find you now have eleven.
Next eat the brown. Go on, eat all seven!

$$\begin{array}{r} 11 \\ -\ 7 \\ \hline 4 \end{array}$$

Now you have four left. So please eat the green.
The orange, red and yellow still can be seen.

$$4 - 1 \over 3$$

Next eat the orange one, and after you do . . .
How many are left? Oh dear, only two!

$$\begin{array}{r} 3 \\ -1 \\ \hline 2 \end{array}$$

Now eat the yellow — it's second to last.
Counting like this makes time fly by fast.

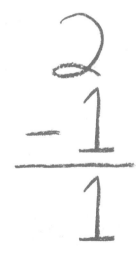

How many are left? You're right. Only one.
Eat the red which is last. Now you are done!

$$\begin{array}{r}1\\-\,1\\\hline 0\end{array}$$

When none are left — it means there are zero.
You've reached the end. You're the grand champion hero!

You've done a great job and I'm so proud of you.
To help you remember, here's your review!

Colors:

 tan

 green

 brown

 orange

 yellow

 red

Shapes:

 square

 triangle

circle

Numbers:

1 One	2 Two	3 Three
4 Four	5 Five	6 Six
7 Seven	8 Eight	9 Nine
10 Ten	11 Eleven	12 Twelve

The Sets of 12:

1 Set • • • • • • • • • • • •

2 Sets • • • • • •   • • • • • •

3 Sets • • • •   • • • •   • • • •

4 Sets • • •   • • •   • • •   • • •

6 Sets • •   • •   • •   • •   • •   • •